THIS BOOK BELONGS TO

_____

13-Digit ISBN: 978-1604337174
10-Digit ISBN: 1604337176

This book may be ordered by mail from the publisher. Please include $5.99 for postage and handling. Please support your local bookseller first!

Books published by Cider Mill Press Book Publishers are available at special discounts for bulk purchases in the United States by corporations, institutions, and other organizations. For more information, please contact the publisher.

Cider Mill Press Book Publishers
Where good books are ready for press
PO Box 454
12 Spring Street
Kennebunkport, Maine 04046

Visit us on the Web!
www.cidermillpress.com

Cover design by Alicia Freile, Tango Media
Interior design by Alicia Freile, Tango Media
Typography: AT Sackers Roman, Engravers Roman, Georgia

Image credits in order of appearance:
Cover wrap image: Abraham Lincoln facing front (Library of Congress Prints and Photographs Division LC-USZ62-13016); Abraham Lincoln's signature (Wikimedia Commons); front endpapers: Birthplace of Abraham Lincoln in Hardin County, Kentucky (Everett Historical /Shutterstock.com), and Abraham Lincoln facing front (Library of Congress Prints and Photographs Division LC-USZ62-13016); "Nicolay Copy" of the Gettysburg Address, 1863 (Library of Congress Digital ID# al0186p1); Abraham Lincoln holding rope of flag (Library of Congress Prints and Photographs Division LC-USZ62-13016); Abraham Lincoln at Antietam, October 3, 1862. (Everett Historical /Shutterstock.com); Abraham Lincoln returning to his Springfield home (Everett Historical /Shutterstock.com); Abraham Lincoln, candidate for U.S. president, before delivering his Cooper Union address in New York City (Library of Congress Prints and Photographs Division LC-USZ62-5803); The manuscript of the Preliminary Emancipation Proclamation (Everett Historical / Shutterstock.com); Abraham Lincoln depicted as a frontier rail splitter in 1909 commemorative portrait. (Everett Historical /Shutterstock.com); Allegorical print of Lincoln emancipated the slaves in 1870 print commemorating the Emancipation Proclamation (Everett Historical /Shutterstock.com); Abraham Lincoln (Everett Historical /Shutterstock.com); Abraham Lincoln, 'rail-splitter,' chromolithograph 1897(Everett Historical /Shutterstock.com); Illustration depicting Abraham Lincoln reading to his family, c. 1860s. (Everett Historical /Shutterstock.com); Abraham Lincoln and his son Tad looking at an album of photographs (Library of Congress Prints and Photographs Division LC-USZ62-11897); Statue of Abraham Lincoln reading while riding horse in Chiang Rai, Thailand (Have a nice day Photo /Shutterstock.com); Statue of President Lincoln in Lincoln Memorial (Steve Heap /Shutterstock.com); back endpapers: Abraham Lincoln portrait of June 3, 1860 by Alexander Hesler (Everett Historical /Shutterstock.com) and Abraham Lincoln Springfield House (Nagel Photography/ Shutterstock.com).

Printed in China

1 2 3 4 5 6 7 8 9 0
First Edition

ABRAHAM LINCOLN

NOTEBOOK

CIDER MILL PRESS

BOOK
PUBLISHERS
KENNEBUNKPORT, MAINE

Introduction

BY MIM HARRISON

On November 2, 1863, a young attorney acting as an agent for Pennsylvania's governor wrote a letter to Abraham Lincoln, inviting him to speak at the consecration of the Civil War battleground at Gettysburg. The President would not be delivering the oration—that would be the purview of the Honorable Edward Everett. Rather, President Lincoln was to deliver "a few appropriate remarks."

For the most part, the world has little noted nor long remembered the author of that letter (David Wills), but the "few appropriate remarks" that Abraham Lincoln delivered on November 19, 1863, are embedded in the American psyche. Most of us can call up from memory some of the scant two hundred seventy-two words of the Gettysburg

Address. The day following Lincoln's delivery, Edward Everett—who was considered the country's foremost orator—wrote Lincoln a letter. "I should be glad," he stated, "if...I came as near to the central idea of the occasion, in two hours, as you did in two minutes."

"Short, short, short" was how Lincoln had earlier described the address he was carefully and laboriously crafting. Although it wasn't always this way.

In 1854, Lincoln gave a pivotal speech in Peoria, Illinois, criticizing the Kansas-Nebraska Act and denouncing slavery. On this occasion, Lincoln outspoke Everett, delivering a three-hour-long discourse. Even so, the speech played well because of its impassioned eloquence.

One of Lincoln's many gifts was that he spoke with his mind, his heart, and his ear, often reading his speeches aloud to a friend or family member before delivering them. "Read it slowly," he once advised a colleague who was presenting a speech he had written but could not deliver.

But even Lincoln had his learning curves. An 1893 biographer, John T. Morse Jr., wrote wryly: "Of Lincoln's [1840] speeches only one has been preserved, and it leads to the conclusion that nothing of value was lost when the others perished."

Yet by the time of the Lincoln-Douglas debates in 1858, this same biographer was writing admiringly of Lincoln's speeches: "Each sentence has its special errand."

A PRESIDENT POETICAL

Lincoln, as his stepmother told another of his biographers, his law partner William Herndon, "was diligent for Knowledge" from an early age. And he once declared that writing, "the art of communicating thoughts to the mind, through the eye," was the world's leading invention.

Two of the earliest books Lincoln studied were Samuel Kirkham's *English Grammar* and William Scott's *Lessons in Elocution,* which contained Shakespearean soliloquies. His own earliest writings, starting in his teenage years, were poems. Some were light verse, other were melancholy. Although he abandoned any notion of becoming a full-time poet, the rhythm and cadence of the **form** stayed with him. They are in part why we react with our hearts as well as our heads when we encounter the Gettysburg Address. In fact, some Lincoln scholars describe the Gettysburg Address as a "prose poem."

Both of Lincoln's Inaugural Addresses are also filled with language that elevates and resonates— the "mystic chords of memory" and "better angels of our nature" from his address of March 4, 1861, and "[w]ith malice toward none; with charity for all" from his address of March 4, 1865. In all of these instances, Lincoln acknowledges the issues of the day and then transcends them, his language infusing them with timelessness and universality. The Gettysburg Address, for example, never references Gettysburg. Instead, "We are met on a great battlefield...." But when necessary, Lincoln could also draw from his experience in practicing law, as he did in composing the deliberately specific, legalistic language of the Emancipation Proclamation.

One thing he frequently drew from, regardless of the subject matter, was his hat.

ENLIGHTENING

For a short time in his early working life, Lincoln served, somewhat indifferently, as postmaster in New Salem, Illinois. His delivery method consisted of putting any incoming letters in his hat, then passing them out as he happened to see their recipients. He soon dropped the job but not the use of his hat. Now, however, it would become the repository of history.

Lincoln was known to jot down ideas on small slips of paper that he would then toss into his hat. It may have been another manifestation of his tendency

Our cause, then, must be intrusted to, and conducted by its own undoubted friends—

THOSE WHOSE HANDS ARE FREE, WHOSE HEARTS ARE IN THE WORK

—who *do care* for the result.

—*"House Divided" speech* (June 16, 1858)

from younger days to write out passages from books that he wished to remember, on whatever writing surface was available. Eventually Lincoln would retrieve the various notes from his hat, sometime numbering them sequentially. So he did, quite literally, pull ideas out of his hat.

The nineteen-foot statue of a seated Lincoln that fills the Lincoln Memorial serves as a metaphor for the language of Lincoln—it towers and soars. Daniel Chester French was the sculptor. Among his collection of letters in the Library of Congress is a series of them addressing how important it was to properly light the sculpture. The Memorial, like the man, serves as a beacon. Lincoln's words will indeed be long remembered, and even longer cherished.

The first page of the "Nicolay Copy" of the Gettysburg Address, the earliest known draft.

WE SHALL NOT FAIL

—if we stand firm,
we shall not fail.

—*"House Divided" speech*
(June 16, 1858)

Abraham Lincoln

We are not enemies, but friends.

WE MUST NOT BE ENEMIES.

Though passion may have strained, it must not break our bonds of affection. The mystic chords of memory...will yet swell the chorus of the Union, when again touched, as surely they will be, by the better angels of our nature.

—First Inaugural Address (March 4, 1861)

With malice toward none; with charity for all...
LET US STRIVE ON TO FINISH THE WORK
we are in...to do all which may achieve and
cherish a just, and a lasting peace, among
ourselves, and with all nations.

—*Second Inaugural Address* (March 4, 1865)

Abraham Lincoln at Antietam with Col. Alexander S. Webb, Gen. George B. McClellan, Scout Adams, and Dr. Jonathan Letterman, October 3, 1862.

—that this nation, under
God, shall have a new birth of
freedom—and that government

OF THE PEOPLE,
BY THE PEOPLE,
FOR THE PEOPLE,

shall not perish from the earth.

—*Gettysburg Address* (November 19, 1863)

Abraham Lincoln returning to his Springfield home after his successful campaign for the Presidency of the United States, in October, 1860.

I do not mean to say that this
government is charged with
the duty of redressing or
preventing all the wrongs in the
world; but I do think that
IT IS CHARGED WITH
the duty of preventing
and redressing
**ALL WRONGS WHICH
ARE WRONGS TO
ITSELF.**

—*Speech at Cincinnati, Ohio* (September 17, 1859)

Let us have faith that

RIGHT MAKES MIGHT,

and in that faith, let us,
to the end, dare to do our duty
as we understand it.

—*Cooper Union Address* (February 27, 1860)

Abraham Lincoln, candidate for U.S. president,
before delivering his Cooper Union Address

TOWERING GENIUS DISTAINS A BEATEN PATH.

It seeks regions hitherto unexplored.

—*Lyceum Address* (January 27, 1838)

...that on the first day of
January, in the year of
our Lord one thousand
eight hundred and sixty-three,
all persons held as slaves
SHALL BE THEN,
THENCEFORWARD,
AND FOREVER
FREE.

—*Emancipation Proclamation* (January 1, 1863)

The manuscript of the Preliminary Emancipation Proclamation

By the President of the United States of America

A Proclamation.

Whereas, on the twenty-second day of September, in the year of our Lord one thousand eight hundred and sixty-two, a proclamation was issued by the President of the United States, containing, among other things, the following, to wit:

"That on the first day of January, in the year of our Lord one thousand eight hundred and sixty-three, all persons held as slaves within any State or designated part of a State, the people whereof shall then be in rebellion against the United States, shall be then, thenceforward, and forever free; and the Executive Government of the United States, including the military and naval authority thereof, will recognize and maintain the freedom of such persons, and will do no act or acts to repress such persons, or any of them, in any efforts they may make for their actual freedom.

"That the Executive will, on the first day

May our children and our children's children to a thousand generations, continue to **ENJOY THE BENEFITS CONFERRED UPON US BY A UNITED COUNTRY,** and have cause yet to rejoice under those glorious institutions bequeathed us by Washington and his compeers.

—*Speech at Frederick, Maryland* (October 4, 1862)

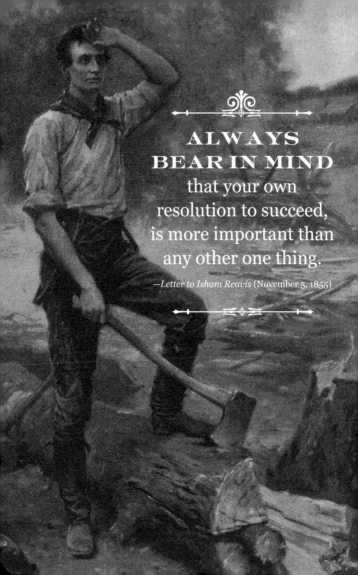

ALWAYS BEAR IN MIND that your own resolution to succeed, is more important than any other one thing.

—*Letter to Isham Reavis* (November 5, 1855)

Allegorical 1870 print of Lincoln emancipated the slaves as proclaimed on the 22nd September 1862.

I have never had a feeling
politically that did not

SPRING FROM THE
SENTIMENTS

embodied in the Declaration
of Independence.

—*Address in Independence Hall, Philadelphia* (February 22, 1861)

EVERY BLADE OF GRASS IS A STUDY;

and to produce two, where there was but one, is both a profit and a pleasure.

—Address before the Wisconsin State Agricultural Society
(September 30, 1859)

Abraham Lincoln

THOSE WHO DENY FREEDOM TO OTHERS,

deserve it not for themselves.

—Letter to Henry L. Pierce et al. (April 6, 1859)

ADHERE TO
YOUR PURPOSE
and you will soon feel as well
as you ever did.

—Letter to Quintin Campbell (June 28, 1862)

LINCOLN, RAIL-SPLITTER.

God bless the women
of America!

—*Remarks at Closing of Sanitary Fair,
Washington D.C.* (March 18, 1864)

Illustration depicting Abraham Lincoln reading to his family, c. 1860s.

...we must think anew, and act anew....

—Second Annual Message to Congress (December 1, 1862)

I happen temporarily to occupy this big
White House. I am living witness that
**ANY ONE OF YOUR CHILDREN
MAY LOOK TO COME HERE**
as my father's child has.

—*Speech to the One Hundred Sixty-sixth Ohio Regiment*
(August 22, 1864)

*Abraham Lincoln and his son Tad looking at
an album of photographs*

It is not merely for today,
but for all time to come that
we should perpetuate for our
children's children

THIS GREAT
AND FREE
GOVERNMENT,

which we have enjoyed
all our lives.

—Speech to the One Hundred Sixty-sixth Ohio Regiment
(August 22, 1864)

*A statue of Abraham Lincoln reading while riding horse
in Chiang Rai, Thailand*

Abraham Lincoln
his hand and pen

HE WILL BE
GOOD BUT
god knows When

—Lincoln as a poet...and a teenager

I leave you, hoping that
the lamp of liberty will burn in
your bosoms until there shall
no longer be a doubt that

ALL MEN ARE
CREATED FREE
AND EQUAL.

—*Speech at Chicago, Illinois* (July 10, 1858)

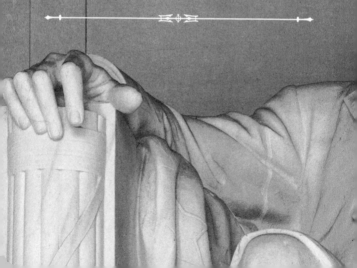

The Lincoln Memorial

About Cider Mill Press
Book Publishers

Good ideas ripen with time. From seed to harvest, Cider Mill Press brings fine reading, information, and entertainment together between the covers of its creatively crafted books. Our Cider Mill bears fruit twice a year, publishing a new crop of titles each spring and fall.

Visit us on the web at
www.cidermillpress.com
or write to us at
12 Spring Street
PO Box 454
Kennebunkport, Maine 04046